...cleverly crafted and overflowing with idiosyncratic characters and mordant humor.
   Killing Adonis reviewed in *Kirkus Reviews* (starred review)

Killing Adonis is the book that Agatha Christie and Tim Burton would have written together.
   Killing Adonis reviewed by *the NSW Writers' Centre*

This creative, original work reminds us we are indeed stardust and that our own diurnal round is a part of a common humanity and a common universe.
   Inter reviewed in *Stage Diary*

...transcendent with the interweaving of poetry and science, past and present.
   We Are All Ghosts reviewed in the *Westender*

Anecdotal and strange, he uses the language of an American comedian with a sort of British wit.
   A Beginner's Guide to Dying in India reviewed in *Four Thousand Magazine*

A+. A Totally Awesome and Magical Book
   Zeb and the Great Ruckus reviewed at *My R and R Space*

Books like this are the reason I read.
   Zeb and the Great Ruckus reviewed at *Batch of Books*

19 ½ Spells Disguised as Poems

by Josh Donellan

with illustrations by
Holly Eastwood

Published by Odyssey Books in 2019
www.odysseybooks.com.au

Copyright © Josh Donellan 2019
www.jmdonellan.com

Illustrations Copyright © Holly Eastwood 2019

All rights reserved. No part of this book may be reproduced or transmitted by any person or entity, including internet search engines or retailers, in any form or by any means, electronic or mechanical, including photocopying (except under the statutory exceptions provisions of the *Australian Copyright Act* 1968), recording, scanning or by any information storage and retrieval system without the prior written permission of the publisher.

A Cataloguing-in-Publication entry is available from the National Library of Australia

ISBN: 978-1-925652-89-5 (pbk)
ISBN: 978-1-925652-90-1 (ebook)

*audio recordings of these poems (spells) are available at
jmdonellan.com/spells*

by the same author

NOVELS
A Beginner's Guide to Dying in India
Killing Adonis

FOR YOUNGER READERS
Zeb and the Great Ruckus

PODCASTS
Six Cold Feet

THEATRE
Inter
We Are All Ghosts

POETRY
Stendhal Syndrome

Contents

A note from the author	ix
The wondrous, miraculous story of why I can't show you my homework	1
My grandma loves hip-hop	4
My (after)life as a zombie	7
A brief explanation of why that box is moving and making strange noises that sound curiously similar to what my little brother would sound like if he was trapped in a box	10
The octopus	13
Crushin' Russian	17
Library	22
An apology to my annoying, stinky brother for breaking your toy laser gun that I only wrote because Mum made me	26
My school tuckshop	28
A poem about my human	30
A poem about my dog	33
Things I want to be when I grow up	36
The mantis shrimp	38

The lie	42
I don't want to analyse this poem	46
The pencil poem	48
A list of things I'd rather do than homework	52
A plane explanation	54
Questions for santa	56
Something something and the amazing whatever*	61
About the author	65
About the illustrator	66

A note from the author

Quick, read this bit before your parents ask what you're looking at! It's *very* important that you know that this whole book is actually a collection of spells very extremely cleverly disguised as poems. You might have noticed that we use the word 'spell' to describe creating words as well as creating magic. That's because words are magical, especially the ones in this book. These spells might save you from great danger someday. So if your parents tell you they don't think it's a good idea to read this book because the author is apparently a weirdo who lives in an underground cave where he is assembling an army of evil robots, you must do *whatever it takes* to convince them otherwise.

Parents are usually right about most things, like eating your vegetables, wearing sunscreen, and not putting your cousin's teddy bear in the toilet. But it's important to remember they can sometimes make terrible mistakes. I mean, look at what they're wearing for crying out loud.

Best fishes,
Josh Donellan

THE WONDROUS, MIRACULOUS STORY OF WHY I CAN'T SHOW YOU MY HOMEWORK

Well, I suppose the whole thing's rather complicated
no, of course I'm not going to tell you that my silly dog ate it
it's a tangled mystery, complex and sophisticated!
the kind of thing that would confuse detectives and secret agents

I had my homework all ready and finished and checked
it was sitting there, right on my desk
when I heard an odd knocking on my bedroom window
and then a strange voice speaking some foreign lingo

I opened the window (and I *swear* this is true)
there was a mystical creature of the strangest hue
a greenishy-yellowy-purpley-sort-of-gold
his breath was quite warm
and he spoke loud and bold

He said, "Human, I am in the gravest of danger!
the gravest danger that you could ever imagine
a danger so grave it is graver than the gravest of grave
the gravest..." (I mean, he went on like this for what felt like an age)

Josh Donellan

"An ancient curse had been cast on my kind!
A curse that can't be undone by magic or time
the only way to save us, and I know this sounds wild
is to offer the homework of a small human child!

I require work that is thoughtful, clever and prudent
the finest work, by the most studious student!
Nothing else will suffice, the curse will still hold
unless the homework is *perfect*!" (or so I was told)

So I ask you, what else could I possibly do?
I couldn't turn him away! I mean, come on, would you?
Even as I handed it over, I was aware of the risk
I knew that you'd be angry, that you'd be seriously...annoyed

In return the mystical visitor commemorated our pact
with the gift of this sacred amulet, here, it's a fact!
Yes, it's true, the paint's still wet and it is made of cardboard
but in the strange stranger's mystical land
that's just what they use for their most sacred artworks

So you see, although my homework is gone, I made a great sacrifice!
I was bolder than bold! Braver than brave! Nicer than nice!
What! I can't believe you'd be so cruel as to call me a liar!
Just because my last homework story included a tragic, homework-targeting fire
and my last before that mysterious, homework-stealing spiders

19½ Spells Disguised as Poems

and the one before that
something about dropping my homework in the large
hadron collider?
and the one before that— ok, if you insist, I'll stop
and I *promise* tonight I'll do my homework *the minute* I get
home

(although the weather report did mention an impending cyclone)

This is a spell to defeat an angry dragon
*Simply write it out on a piece of extra strong paper, fold it
into a paper plane and throw it at the offending beast. In
the unlikely event this does not work, employ an emergency
retreat protocol (run like crazy).*

MY GRANDMA LOVES HIP-HOP

My grandma loves hip-hop
she likes Tupac and Snoop Dogg and Kendrick and Biggie
24/7 she's gettin' down gettin' jiggy
she likes to bust moves yeah she likes to get busy
catch her at the nursing home yelling
"Yo, let's party! Who's with me?"

Her friends Mavis and Gertrude and Bessie and Baz
all prefer classical and piano jazz
but whenever they play it, Nan says, "THIS IS AS BORING AS STATIC!"
then she throws on the classic Nas album, *Illmatic*

She cruises the streets in her rusty Corolla
bumping the Roots, people watch and they holler
she raps along to every word to every verse to every song
my grandma spits lyrics till the break of dawn

Mum says she wishes grandma would just act her age
but Nan says though she's old she's still filled with passion and rage
she says:
"I'm gonna spend my last breath blasting sucka MCs
I might have a bad back and terrible knees
but I spit slick syllables with phenomenal ease
guaranteed to keep it hot like 100 degrees

I like phat beats for breakfast and brunch and afternoon tea
verbal assassin cutting whack rappers like chainsaws cut trees
my lyrical skill is pure top pedigree
my poetry's so potent it incites riots and parts the red sea!"

Nan just had her 80th birthday
she played nothing but hip-hop
she gathered the family around and yelled
"Yo DJ, let the beat drop!"

Then she busted moves with her new artificial hip
she cut up the rug with her moves so slick
the kids were like, "Wow, Grandma's skills are totally sick!"
and we all dropped our jaws when she landed a backflip

Some say my nan's a very twisted individual
she's thoroughly obsessed with everything that's lyrical
but she says she's just living life at its peak, at its pinnacle
and it's everybody else who needs to reassess their principles

Some people might think my nan is a little bit strange
that she's got mental problems, that her age is to blame
but she's living her life with passion and vigour and fire
and when I get old I wanna be just like her

This is a spell to make your parents tell you to be quiet
Simply recite this spell (poem) as loud as you possibly can and it should work almost immediately. <u>Note:</u> use this spell sparingly; it can have dangerous side effects such as getting grounded or being denied dessert.

MY (AFTER)LIFE AS A ZOMBIE

I used to be human
Yes, really, it's true!
I used to be human
almost exactly like you
I used to brush my teeth and eat spaghetti for dinner
but now I'm a zombie and my life is quite different

I wake every evening from the grave where I sleep
and go searching for delicious brains to savour and eat
I like them juicy and tender and slimy and sweet
I find noisy young children have the tastiest cranial treats

Though I smell awful and my flesh is all rotten
my clothes are falling apart and my name's been forgotten
my skin has turned green
and my hair's a disaster
my eyes keep falling out
and my teeth are the colour of Parisian plaster

I can't complain, being undead is quite fetching
I start my day with meditation and then yoga stretching
I water my plants, and play with all of my action figures
then I go in search of brains to have for my dinner

Josh Donellan

I don't have to go to work
or see the doctor or dentist
I don't have to pay bills
or pretend I care about football or opera or tennis
I can at last live a life (or afterlife?) that is truly authentic

To keep myself busy
I've joined a goth-rock band (I play the bass)
we write songs about bats and spiders and space
the others all wear costumes and make-up and masks
I just show up looking like normal
and the whole crowd collectively gasps

I used to be a tax accountant
I was constantly bored
but now I rock out on stage
with a look that can't be ignored

I eat brains for lunch, dinner, and breakfast
and I play bass in rock clubs
with my bandmates Joy, Raj, and Cedric

I used to be human
yes, really, it's true!
but now I'm a zombie
and life's much improved

19½ Spells Disguised as Poems

This is a spell to ward off zombies
Simply say it once a week, and zombies will keep well away. Very useful if you enjoy having a brain and do not want it to be eaten.

A BRIEF EXPLANATION OF WHY THAT BOX IS MOVING AND MAKING STRANGE NOISES THAT SOUND CURIOUSLY SIMILAR TO WHAT MY LITTLE BROTHER WOULD SOUND LIKE IF HE WAS TRAPPED IN A BOX

Yes, I absolutely promise!
yes, I'm absolutely sure!
I swear it's not my brother
could you not ask me anymore?

I don't know why it's shaking
I don't know why it roars
I don't know why it's screaming
I could not guess the cause

Why won't you believe me
why do you keep asking?
why do you not trust me?
I feel so offended that it's frightening!

Yes, I'm aware my brother's missing
yes, I know it sounds just like him
but I wouldn't trap him in a box
(although I really do dislike him)

And I surely wouldn't ever
tape said box completely shut
then cover it with a blanket
that would be completely nuts!

He probably went out
for a Sunday evening stroll
and was kidnapped by a pirate
or fell into a hole

Perhaps he's joined the circus
and been eaten by a lion
maybe he became a monk
and wants to live his life in silence

He might have moved to Lima (that's a city in Peru)
or perhaps to the Sahara
I'll surely miss him
and I know that you will too

FINE! I'll take off the pillows and the blanket and the tape
but I really must repeat that I think it's a mistake
I can't be held responsible for what horrors lay inside
and if it's quite all right with you…I think I'll quickly run
and hide

Josh Donellan

This is a spell to make your parents happy
Recite this spell (poem) while cleaning your room and you will notice their mood quickly improves. This spell is often used immediately after the 'Spell To Make Your Parents Tell You To Be Quiet.'

THE OCTOPUS

The octopus has eight arms to hold you
enfold you
but it rarely does what it's told to
a significant portion of the octopus's thinking
happens in its partially autonomous arms
now I don't want to cause you alarm
but that's something which no other creature on earth
can do

its intellectual processing is unique
it is a beautiful freak
and these limbs, eight things
with which it thinks and swims
sing hymns
in sign language

It can accomplish miracles
other creatures could not hope to manage
this cephalopod (quite odd)
is remarkably clever
these oceanic Houdinis can easily escape a closed jar
if you were in the same situation
I bet you wouldn't make it very far
I mean, putting a human being in a giant jar certainly
isn't ethical
and would probably be quite weird

but to be clear
we're only talking hyperbolic hypotheticals here

The octopus, a marine genius
has a lifespan of between two and five years
and in this time they demonstrate complex
observational learning abilities
solving puzzles with eight-armed agility
which is pretty impressive, I suppose
because I don't know about you
but when I was two years old
I was just shoving various objects into my nose
imagine if the octopus lived until eighty?
apart from the fact that this would make it an octopedal octogenarian
its intelligence
if it lived this long
could theoretically rival your average librarian

The octopus has three hearts
I'm going to say that again: *three* hearts
they probably think the John Farnham song
Two Strong Hearts is a tragedy about an individual organism
with a partially malfunctioning cardiovascular system

The octopus uses ink as a weapon
let's just stop...

...and think about that for a second
we all know that the pen is mightier than the sword
and the octopus uses a writing tool as pure and potent metaphor
like: "Damn your wars
I'm going to squirt ink and then escape!
disappear into the night like Batman behind cape
while you hyperventilate and holler
I'll be getting nourished
in the sea, that's where I flourish
chowing down on scallops and some molluscs
using eight arms to write simultaneous soliloquies and sonnets!"

This is a creature clearly too miraculous for
anywhere else but the wondrous world of the ocean's floor
too astonishing for any average aquarium
too confounding for even complex contemplation
a creature so strange and alien
it should probably vacation
on satellites and space stations

The true extent of cephalopod intelligence remains unknown
although we make studies quite thorough
the octopus continues to intrigue everyone from marine biologists
to Sir David Attenborough like:

Josh Donellan

"Here on the ocean floor, lives an eight-armed mystery
And we can truly only guess at its myriad complexities."

This is a spell to transform yourself into an octopus
Recite this poem with one foot in the ocean and one foot on the sand while juggling six slick seashells and balancing a beach ball on your head. <u>Please note:</u> this is a particularly difficult spell and has only been successfully performed eight times in the last 800 years.

CRUSHIN' RUSSIAN

Now picture this, let me just paint the scene
I was in Ecuador, I was living the dream
and one evening I found myself in a strange situation
accidentally ended up in a bar of the criminal persuasion
I should've done my research and sought out local intelligence
because it turns out this place was popular with the illegitimate elements
gangsters and thieves
and the malicious, malevolent

I ended up seated between two monstrous mountains of muscle
they were titans, beasts, goliaths, behemoths
I couldn't squeeze past them or run for the exit
they had arms like footballs squished into skin sacks
eyes like bleak windows into wintertime gulags

The taller giant turned to me
lips peeled back into an insidious leer
and he said in a thick Russian accent
"Puny man, what are you doing here?"
I replied, "Um...just finishing my beer?"

Josh Donellan

He said, "I am a Russian ultimate fighter
they call me the Colossal Cossack
in the ring I cannot be beat
I do not know the meaning of the word 'defeat'!"

I said, "Well, it means the act of being bested or losing
to be overthrown, overturned, overcome
or in a word vanquished—"
he roared "SILENCE!"
I zipped my lips quick, frozen with panic

He snarled and leaned into me
and said leering and sneering
"I could crush your tiny bones into nothing!"
It wasn't a threat so much as a statement of fact
and I didn't know how to respond or react
I imagined those meat hammer fists smashing my skull
my body broken and bruised, beaten red, blue and black
I pictured the newspaper headline:
Aussie Tourist Gets Concussion From Crushin' Russian's Attack!

The giant grunted
an exhalation that was positively primeval, reptilian
the kind of noise rarely issued from the mouths of civilised civilians
I imagined his defeated enemies, numbering millions upon millions
he probably ate babies for breakfast
and supped on the souls of supervillains

I was desperate, confused, afraid, terrified
I summoned my courage
and looked him straight in the eye
I inhaled

                          and proceeded to stammer:
"I get it, you're the Colossal Cossack with fists like meat hammers
you could kill me quicker than ten dozen daggers
you could grind my flesh into a tangle of tatters
the bards would sing of your ignoble infamy
but please crushin' Russian
tell me what it is that you *want* from me?"

His face flared a bright, communist red
I closed my eyes and waited for the onslaught of death
or at least to wake up in a hospital bed
but there was no pain, no violence forthcoming
just a quiet, distraught Russian
snifflin' and snufflin'

He was torn apart, come undone
his words transformed into tiny tombstones
tumbling forth from the tip of his trembling tongue

Josh Donellan

He whispered:
"I can hurl boulders
break bricks
crush bones
there is nothing and no one who can stand above me
but all I really want
is for my daughter to love me!

She doesn't write
doesn't email
never calls!
my beautiful Natasha
she treats me like a stranger
and leaves me alone with my sadness and anger

I am ruthless, unstoppable inside of the ring
but the truth is all of this strength, it means not a thing
I feel useless and toothless like old, broken string
I am adored by my fans, but ignored by my kin."

I watched the mountain of muscle
dissolve like a Panadol placed in cold water
at the thought of his strange and estranged daughter
I watched him crumple, crumble and break
then squeezed my way past and made my escape

And some days when I feel lost, lonely, on the brink
I think of my discussion with the crushin' Russian
crying into his drink

19½ Spells Disguised as Poems

I lay back, soak up those warm thoughts, relax and then think
I'm grateful for those who love me
the strength they grant to this fragile, flimsy, fracturable writer
but most of all?
I'm grateful I wasn't beaten to death by a crushin' Russian ultimate fighter

This is a spell to make a new friend
Write this spell (poem) out on some pretty paper in your very neatest handwriting, then place it in an envelope which you've decorated with your very best art. Also include a note saying something along the lines of 'I think you're very ____ and extremely ____. Would you like to be my friend and play ____?' This spell may take time to work, but is extra effective if you include a party invitation and/or lollipop.

LIBRARY

When I was a kid I lived in a house with four walls and one door
and not much more
and we often ate food raw
because the oven was usually broken
and our voices were often softly spoken
because the walls were thin
and the floor had holes that I would often fall in

I would sit there surrounded by a hidden stash of books
and I would be there
quiet as death
soft as breath
still as stone
in that place where no one could find me
and I would read and read and read
all the books that I got from the
library

When I was a kid I had two shirts that I alternated daily
they were old and faded
and like my home dilapidated
but I never minded that my home was an eyesore
because I saw many other homes
every time I stepped through the library door
I had houses in Rivendell

and Narnia and deepest darkest Africa
and Gotham city and in Metropolis
and the Faraway Tree and Wonderland and
I would go on vacation to Never Never Land
and I could transform at will into Peter Pan
and Spiderman
in the library

When I was a teenager
I had one dream:
to become a writer
I was a skinny kid with a huge imagination
because I didn't have time for push-ups
(although I did make time for PlayStation)

I was just a dorky kid with glasses
and sometimes I'd get beat up between classes
and sometimes I'd come home and my parents would be fighting
and sometimes my grades would be downright frightening
and sometimes I'd confuse the right thing and the wrong thing
but between the pages I'd feel safe
and I could always find happy endings
and sad ones too
because life isn't always happy
and stories shouldn't be either

Josh Donellan

So I sat there with my head between pages
just soaking up stories for ages and ages
about witches and warlocks and mages
about faraway places and where the end of space is
about worlds that could be
once were
or should have been
and the library held innumerable portals to unknown dreams
and the librarians were gatekeepers
who passed me the keys
to all of these stories in the books that I'd read
and I read Margaret Atwood and Salman Rushdie
and I felt like nothing in this or any other world could stop me
and it took time and it took hard work
but eventually the day came
when I found my own book
sitting on that shelf in the library

And I like to imagine some kid
maybe skinny like me
or maybe different, completely
sliding my book down into their little hands
beneath those bright white lights
putting my story into their eyes
and their imaginations lighting up like an Olympic torch
then taking a pen and scribbling their thoughts
and in that garden of knowledge a new idea being born
and that kid watching it grow and listening to the sounds of their brainstorm

that little kid has a home
just like mine
and it's spelled L-I-B-R-A-R-Y

This is a spell to make everything in the universe simultaneously double in size
Put on clothes that are at least 6 sizes too big for you and say this spell (poem) in your loudest voice. Close your eyes, count to 19 and a half, and when you open them everything in the universe (including you) will have precisely doubled in size!

AN APOLOGY TO MY ANNOYING, STINKY BROTHER FOR BREAKING YOUR TOY LASER GUN THAT I ONLY WROTE BECAUSE MUM MADE ME

I'm sorry I squished it
and stomped it
and ran over it
with my digger truck's tyres

Then threw it at the wall
picked it up
and set it on fire

I'm sorry I dropped it from the balcony
then hung it from wires
then pulled it apart
with rusty old pliers

I'm sorry I kicked it
and chucked it
and boiled it
I'm sorry I threw it into the bin
and then into the toilet

19½ Spells Disguised as Poems

I'm sorry it's now broken to pieces
and completely useless
it was all an accident
I didn't do it on purpose!

So forgive me, won't you, will you, please?

PS you smell like stinky old cheese

This is a spell to travel (slowly) through time
Say it forwards once quickly, then backwards slowly, then three more times at normal speed while turning in a clockwise circle. From now on you will travel very slowly forward into the future (at a rate of roughly one second per second).

MY SCHOOL TUCKSHOP

My school tuckshop's better than yours
my school tuckshop's better because
while yours might serve sandwiches and such
icy poles and fruit and other stuff
mine serves cuisine that is somewhat stranger
it's delivered in boxes that are marked 'danger'

For morning tea, for example
I might eat a small and delightful sample
of catguts and of newt entrails
with a side of sautéed snails

And if I'm still hungry I just might
indulge in a piece of Turkish delight
however, this stuff is of a particular variety
(it's made from turkey eyeballs, just quietly)

My favourite dish, however
is as strange as I am clever
yes, the dish that I adore the most
is spicy monkey brains on toast

Although I confess I'm also fond
of sea slugs served up on palm fronds
of pies made with delicious worms
and soup made from the feet of birds

19½ Spells Disguised as Poems

The lunch lady is said to be part demon
with yellow fangs and eyes deep crimson
she serves our food with a frightening leer
and there's a rumour going on round here

That the most horrible, despicable
and repulsive of children
sent to the principal's office one too many times
for one too many heinous crimes
are subsequently
and swiftly delivered
to the lunch lady, who then makes them into dinner

So I'm not so keen on the hamburgers you see
because I'm afraid they're made out of my friend Louise

This is a spell to make ice-cream 12% more delicious
Recite this spell (poem) very S-L-O-W-L-Y fifteen minutes before eating ice-cream. If you are vegan or lactose intolerant, it may also work on your favourite pasta.

A POEM ABOUT MY HUMAN
(by Pickle the dog)

My human's my best friend!
Best companion!
Best mate!
Everything she does is amazing and fantastic and super and great!

She feeds me and bathes me and protects me from storms!
She keeps me happy and healthy and well-fed and warm!

We're best friends, it's true, we are!
We—
Hang on, I just need to go chase this car

Okay! That mean car is gone, I scared it right off!
It won't be back again, I showed it who's boss!
Now where was I?

Oh yes! My human (her name is Amy)
I think she's the greatest
And really, who'd blame me?

She plays with me and walks with me and takes me outside
Have you been outside before? *Man,* what a ride!
EVERYTHING OUT THERE IS SO AMAZING!
THERE ARE SO MANY SMELLS, IT MAKES ME GO CRAZY!
There's roses and footpath and food and dirt to smell
Sometimes there's dead possums, I love that smell as well!

I love Amy
I help her in oh so many ways
100% of the time
Every hour, every day

Sometimes I help her by chewing her shoes
Sometimes I help her by eating her food
Sometimes I help her by scaring off dudes
Sometimes by covering the kitchen with glue

I love her, adore her
She's perfect, sublime
She loves me too
100% of the time

Even though she's not very hairy, and only two-legged
I think she's perfect, there is no one better
I am her dog
She is my human
It's a perfect, incredible, astonishing union

Josh Donellan

This is a spell to make puppies very slightly more adorable
I know, I didn't think it was possible either, but try it for yourself! Simply say this poem while staring directly at a puppy and it should work almost instantly!

A POEM ABOUT MY DOG
(by Amy the human)

My dog's my best friend!
Best canine!
Best pal!
Everything she does is filled with ZOOM and BAM and POW!

I feed her and bathe her and protect her from storms
She keeps me happy and safe and relaxed and calm

We're best friends, it's true, we are!
We—
Hang on, she's running after a car

Okay, I chased her and brought her away from the road
It was partly my fault, I forgot the gate wasn't properly closed
Now where was I?

Josh Donellan

Oh yes, my dog (her name is Pickle)
I think she's the greatest
She is without equal

She comes with me to the park where I play on the slide
And swing on the swings while she runs and hides
I fly my kite and dig in the sandpit while Pickle digs up dead possums
They smell like grandma's toilet, UGH! So disgusting!
We smell roses and laugh at clouds and draw on the footpath
And then we come home, in time to make word art

I love Pickle
Even though she can be so crazy
In so many ways
It truly does amaze me

Sometimes she makes me mad by chewing my shoes
Sometimes she helps me by chewing gross food
Sometimes she barks at my friend Jimmy (she can be very rude)
One time she covered the kitchen in a tub of craft glue

I love her, I squish her
She's magic, she's mine
I absolutely adore her
98% of the time

19½ Spells Disguised as Poems

Even though she's messy and crazy and smelly
We go together like ice-cream and jelly
She is my dog
I am her human
It's a perfect, incredible, astonishing union

This is a spell to make your dog less stinky
Recite this poem while bathing your dog. Should take effect straight away. <u>Note:</u> be careful not to get the book wet otherwise it will be ruined and your parents will have to buy another copy and...Actually, go ahead and get it wet if need be, as long as you have a trip to the bookshop planned in the near future.

THINGS I WANT TO BE WHEN I GROW UP

When I grow up I would really truly like to be
the queen of outer space or the king of killer bees
a professional eater of ice-cream and/or of expensive chocolate
a skateboard tester or someone who writes about a great sci-fi apocalypse

A dog trainer trainer
so I could spend all day with people who train dogs
or a hog tamer tamer so I could tame the people who tame hogs
time traveller, space traveller or the secret person who steals socks
Minecrafter, Fortniter or a person who breaks clocks

A seal translator so we could know what those weird fishy things are always saying
a toy tester so I could make sure the toys don't explode during playing
the evil gremlin whom I assume is hiding inside of my dad's laptop
(there must be some reason why he's always yelling at it nonstop)

A warlock, wizard, witch or a zombie who eats brains
a wicked, evil scientist (you know, the kind who's mostly or
even totally insane)

The person who comes up with all the different kinds of
soft drinks
there'd be belly-button flavour
and toe jam flavour
and ogre-vomit flavour too!
there'd be one that tastes like dog farts
and one like muddy shoes

Although I also really love to lie
maybe I should become a politician?
or maybe I could just do sneaky tricks
and be a lawyer or magician

So many choices!
so many options!
who knows what the future holds?
the one thing I can't be anymore is a baby
Mum says I'm just too old

This is a spell to make you grow taller
Recite this spell (poem) while standing on your bed and reaching your fingers up as high as you possibly can. <u>Note:</u> this spell will take several years to work and may have side effects such as growing hair in weird places and experiencing the overwhelming urge to yell, 'YOU DON'T UNDERSTAND!!!!!' at your parents every 10-15 minutes.

THE MANTIS SHRIMP

All my friends want to be lions
monkeys, bears and jungle tyrants
giant predators that prowl and growl and scream
but the animal I most admire
in my mind there's no star brighter
the creature that I think reigns supreme

Is the mantis shrimp

It has eyes that can see many colours
when it comes to vision there's no other
animal on earth that's quite so adept
it can see in ultraviolet
and it can be ultra-violent
it devours, hunts and kills without regret

That's the mantis shrimp

Mantis shrimp
mantis shrimp
rainbow-bright and so deadly
mantis shrimp
mantis shrimp
there's simply none like thee

19½ Spells Disguised as Poems

At the zoo my friends all gather
around gorillas, apes and adders
but to me they're boring, dull and plain
they say, "Look, they jump and climb!"
I say, "I'm off, if you don't mind
in search of creatures that are far less lame."

Like the mantis shrimp

Mantis shrimp
mantis shrimp
rainbow-bright and so deadly
mantis shrimp
mantis shrimp
there's simply none like thee

Its claws can move so lightning fast!
they can heat water and also break glass
don't even try to keep them in a tank
they punch with the force of Superman
they crush their prey with their mighty hands
to make them angry would be a mistake

Don't annoy a mantis shrimp!

Mantis shrimp
mantis shrimp
rainbow-bright and so deadly
mantis shrimp
mantis shrimp
there's simply none like thee

Josh Donellan

So, when next asked your favourite creature
make sure that your answer's either
the mantis shrimp or perhaps something even more insane
(like the tardigrade)
and when they respond in horror
clutch their pearls, and loosen collars
you can go ahead and sing its name:

Mantis shrimp
mantis shrimp
rainbow-bright and so deadly
mantis shrimp
mantis shrimp
there's simply none like thee

19½ Spells Disguised as Poems

This is a spell to make invisible things stay invisible
Occasionally, invisible things like to suddenly become visible. This, of course, can be quite alarming. It is recommended that someone recites this spell at least once a year to avoid a lot of confusion such as people pointing at things yelling, 'Why can I suddenly see the abstract concept of hope and also why is it a very strange shade of purple?!?'

THE LIE

I told a small lie
it escaped from my mouth
it wrenched my jaws open
and then clawed its way out

I was so surprised
telling a lie was so easy
I just said the words and then my parents believed me!
I thought for sure they'd interrogate me like the police on TV
why'd I bother telling the truth for so long
when I could just as easily
tell a lie, a teeny tiny deception
that would be met with a surprisingly warm and welcome reception?

The lie started out small
insignificant, minuscule, tiny
but whenever I turned around
it was there
it followed so close behind me

It followed me to school
and then it slept in my desk
I could barely pay attention
to the day's spelling test

19½ Spells Disguised as Poems

As the day went on
the lie grew larger and larger as it lumbered behind me
it cast a shadow from the gym all the way to the library
It grew new tentacles, horns, claws, and sharp teeth
It became a gigantic, titanic, calamitous beast

I tried to forget about it
but it found a million ways to remind me
when I walked home I could sense it all horrid and smelly and slimy
with each terrible step it shook the whole earth
with its enormous mass and remarkable girth

It cracked concrete and rustled the leaves of the trees
it now stood so tall, my head barely reached to its knees
when I arrived home it couldn't even fit through the door
it screamed and it hollered and it screeched and it roared

My mother ran downstairs, fuming, and she began pleading
"What's all this commotion and yelling and screaming?
you made so much noise, I thought you'd surely be bleeding
or perhaps there'd been an unexpected limb amputation
by a crocodile or dragon or rabid Alsatian!"

I told her no, no there was no need for an emergency medical service
the problem I was having was a moral disturbance
I closed my eyes, and then I drew in my breath
I clenched my fists, felt my heart race, and then I confessed

Josh Donellan

my mother's face flared red as her eyes lit up with violent volcanoes
she screamed and she hollered and she screeched and she roared
just like my lie had done, merely minutes before

But amongst all the chaos and fury and panic
I noticed something strange: the lie had now vanished
and now as punishment I've been grounded for two whole, long weeks
and although I feel so guilty I'm not sure I can sleep
I'm glad I came clean and at last told the truth
but for now I just lie awake and stare at the cold, distant moon
I won't be lying again, at least not any time soon

19½ Spells Disguised as Poems

This is a spell to make someone who is cross with you forgive you more quickly
Climb under the covers with a torch and say this spell (poem) very quietly, then go into the kitchen and cook them pancakes. It should work as soon as the pancakes reach their bellies.

I DON'T WANT TO ANALYSE THIS POEM

I don't want to analyse this poem
I don't want to slice it small into pieces
I don't want to underline metaphors
and circle where the emotional peak is

I want to absorb it
consume it
and make it a part of me
feel it in my bones and my toes and arteries
I want it to join with my dreams and my memories
to swim around and around with my fears and my fantasies

Because if I have to dissect it
I'll take a great poem and wreck it
leaving me sad and dejected
with all those words vivisected

I don't want to reduce it to tiny components
I'd rather leave it as a collection of beautiful moments
it's not a linguistic schematic
it's not a blueprint for the bats that I keep in the attic

19½ Spells Disguised as Poems

A poem should be words woven together to embrace
majesty, mystery
a collection of letters to create a fragment of emotional
history
pen on the page to record our delights and our tragedies
not a scientific procedure conducted with surgical
accuracy

I wouldn't dissect a cake
tear it apart to find the components that make
that sweet delicious taste
I get when I shove it into my face
I would devour it hungrily, greedily
watching what was once outside
now become a part of me

I want to read poems the same way
embrace them completely
and savour the bliss and the anger and misery
I don't want to analyse this poem
and strip away all its glory
I want to absorb it completely, entirely, wholeheartedly
and have all of the metaphor and simile and hyperbole
become tiny, shimmering, glimmering new parts of me

This is a spell to make yourself dizzy
Say this spell (poem) while turning in a circle as fast as you possibly can.

THE PENCIL POEM

HellooOOOOOoo!
I'm so excited to meet you
I'm your new pencil!
I'm here to assist you with drawing and drafting and sketching and stencils

We're going to have adventures!
We're going to have fun!
We're going to create great poems and stories and haikus and puns!

Wait, what are you doing?
Don't zip me up in this cluttered, crammed pencil case
I feel trapped in here, I want to escape!

Your eraser smells weird
And it never stops speaking
And just so you know
Your highlighter is leaking

And what's that ghastly silver thing
With the hole and the blade?
Why would you have that with you
Are you freaking *insane*?

19½ Spells Disguised as Poems

A pencil sharpener?!? Why would you—
No, no, please, keep it away from me!
I'm not even a little bit blunt
Oh lord would you pray for me!

ARGHHHHHH!
The pain! The humiliation! The torture!
Although I'm now slightly sharper
I'm also *much shorter!*

Ok, back to drawing, great
This is just what I live for!
I can't wait to see
What you use me to draw
Get me down on the page
And let's make some magic!

Wait, what are you drawing...? My goodness how *rude*!
What a vile, demeaning, crude illustration!
I can't believe you used me to draw your teacher that way
The shame! The horror! The humiliation!
If she finds out she'll surely command you to use me
To write boring old lines
Why must you abuse me?

Oh great, back in the case with the eraser and ruler
Your ruler's so uptight and pretentious and rude
And your eraser is foul-mouthed and vicious and crude

Josh Donellan

How I dream of the day
When you'll use me to create something beautiful
Till then, I'll wait here
Patient and dutiful
I'll hope for the day when I just may, just might—
Wait, the zipper is opening
I can now see the light!

NOOO, why must you *chew* me!?!
Devour me, munch me
And place me between your teeth?
I yearn for freedom, expression, release!
Ok, ok, is it happening, finally? PLEASE!
By all that's holy I just feel so alive and so free and so brave!
Watch as I dance, pirouette and spin 'cross the page!
Now let's see here, what have you drawn?

I LOVE IT!
You're so talented
An artistic genius!
You must be one of the most brilliant children
In your entire species!

Well, this first day with you
Has been the most incredible journey!
Such highs
Such lows
And it's only two-thirty!
But for now
I've done my part

19½ Spells Disguised as Poems

I really must rest
Let me lie down quietly
Till the Friday maths test

This is a spell to turn a unicorn into a normal horse
Approach the unicorn slowly with your right hand on your left shoulder and your left hand on your head (this gesture is known to be very calming to unicorns). Once you are within earshot, recite this poem in a pirate voice.

A LIST OF THINGS I'D RATHER DO THAN HOMEWORK

1 play with the dog
2 eat a wheel of cheese
3 stand on my head
4 learn to speak Burmese
5 run outside
6 hide in the bushes
7 run inside
8 hit my brother with cushions
9 do a backflip
10 do a backslide
11 do a back kick
12 back up my hard drive
13 eat spaghetti
14 play with Lego
15 throw confetti
16 dress up like a pharaoh
17 eat boogers
18 fight a bear
19 swallow vomit
20 wear pop's bell bottom flares
21 play my Xbox
22 start a brawl
23 pair my mouldy socks
24 anything at all

19½ Spells Disguised as Poems

This is a spell to make scary storms a bit less scary
Say it while wearing your favourite t-shirt, three pairs of socks, two jumpers and some sort of mask. Extra effective if you do it in a silly voice.

A PLANE EXPLANATION

Sir, please, I beg you, try to understand
the plane did not hit you via my intent or command!
yes, it's true I held it right here in my hand
but a magical wind blew it wholly and entirely unplanned!

I was sitting here innocently paying attention
when a certain kid (whose name I'll not mention)
said, "Oi, share one of the planes from your paper plane collection!"
I replied:
"Good sir, I would *remind you* to listen to our esteemed teacher's direction!"

But he pleaded, implored, he begged and he whined
he asked me once, and then twice, then, like, six more times
I felt like if he kept asking I might lose my mind
so, despite my better judgement, I nodded and obliged

I pinched my prized plane between my two fingers
and the unnamed boy smiled and then sniggered
he opened a window, the plane shot like a bullet commanded by trigger
and flew into your head (as I'm sure you remember)

19½ Spells Disguised as Poems

So you see, Sir, I was so enjoying our lesson on fractions!
I really didn't mean to detract from the action
I certainly didn't intend to cause you harm or distress
and I was so looking forward to this afternoon's test!

Alas, the true villain cannot be here named
for tattle-tales, as you know, are frequently maimed
if I break the code of classroom silence
when the lunch bell goes, I'll endure unspeakable violence

So please, instead, accept my most humble apologies
and allow me to resume the role of classroom prodigy
to inspire the others with my hard work and honesty
to provide help and assistance, and if required, perhaps a little light comedy?

No? Very well
whatever you, in your infinite wisdom
deem to be fair
I'll see you at lunch
I'll be the one in the 'poor choices' chair

This is a spell to make a distant stranger's day more pleasant
Say this poem while thinking of unicorns, puppies, rainbows, guitar solos, lollipops, and rocket ships all at the same time. Note: this spell is not immediately practical for your own purposes, but it is a very nice thing to do.

QUESTIONS FOR SANTA

1 How did you get to be so fat?

2 How do you fit down all those chimneys?

3 How many mice could you hide in your beard?

4 How did you get so old?

5 Do you want to get more old, or just stay the same amount of old?

6 I want to put out cookies for you, but also I want to check if you are gluten intolerant? If so I will find some gluten-free cookies. If not I will see if I can put in some extra gluten. Mum says it's good to be tolerant that's what nice people do but she also says that my friend Amy is lactose intolerant but that's fine so I'm a bit confused and I don't really get it.

7 Did you know you accidentally left the receipt for the book you brought me last Christmas in our bin? I kept it for you, just in case you wanted it (but I should mention it's covered in bin juice).

8 Why did you have to buy me a book from the store? Don't your elves make the gifts?

19½ Spells Disguised as Poems

9 Do you pay your elves union wages? Dad says being part of a union is really important because otherwise your boss will try and squeeze you for every last penny but we don't even use pennies in Australia anymore so I'm not sure that that's a very practical idea anyway. Also how hard do you have to squeeze someone before pennies come out of them? I wanted to try on my brother but Mum says I'm not allowed.

10 Why do I have to write you a letter with a pen and paper like it's the olden days? Mum says you have an email address but it's top secret and only parents are allowed to know it but you could tell me and I promise I wouldn't tell any other kids except Lisa and Xi Lin and Kiera P and Kiera S and Mukesh and my soccer team and the enviro club and my neighbour and my cousin and anyone who asks really, really nicely?

11 What's your favourite colour?

12 What's your favourite animal?

13 What's your favourite coloured animal?

14 What is Mrs Claus's first name? Mum says the fact that she's just called "Mrs Claus" is emblematic of the patriarchal narrative that runs through every aspect of our society. A narrative is a story but I don't see how not having a name is a whole story and I looked up "emblematic" and "patriarchal" in the dictionary but I didn't understand the explanations which is dumb because

the whole point of a dictionary is to explain what words mean so if you don't even understand the explanation you should get a refund.

15 Mum says that you watch us to check if we're naughty or nice. Does that mean you're reading our emails and if so isn't that illegal and also I didn't write that really bad one about my teacher last week I was hacked.

16 How come last year when I visited you at the shopping centre you asked me what I wanted for Christmas even though I'd already sent you a letter telling you what I wanted for Christmas? Is your memory going bad in your old age? If so you should use an app to help you remember things. Dad always says, "There's an app for everything these days!" and then mum usually says, "Is there an app to make you stop saying 'there's an app for everything these days!' because if there was I would definitely use it." and then Dad says some grown-up words that I have to pretend I don't know even though I very definitely know all of them.

17 Shelly runs a lemonade stand. She makes $108 selling 72 glasses of lemonade in three hours. How much did she charge for each glass and how much did she make per hour? (If you could answer this question really quickly, like, before my Monday maths homework is due, I would really appreciate it).

19½ Spells Disguised as Poems

This is a spell to make Christmas come sooner
Say this spell (poem) while wearing a Santa hat, and Christmas will be here before you know it! Note: this spell will take a maximum of 364 days to work.

A(nother) note from the author: *I didn't have time to finish this last poem because I was ~~attacked by an ocelot~~ ~~trapped in a dungeon~~ ~~kidnapped by pirates~~ lazy. However, just this once, I am giving you permission to write in this book. I know, I know! You're not usually supposed to write in books like these, but this time it's okay. So go ahead and finish this poem, draw a picture as well if you want to! Then go write some more poems. Write them on paper with pens or on footpaths with chalk or on your dad's face with permanent marker when he's sleeping (I was told by my lawyer to make it very clear that the last bit is a joke so that I don't get sued. So, I am doing that now, then when my lawyer falls asleep I am going to draw on his face with permanent marker).*

Remember: the world needs more poems and you <u>are just the right person</u> to write them!

SOMETHING SOMETHING AND THE AMAZING WHATEVER*
(* title still needs work)

It was a curious day, to say the least
the kind of day that sees monsters unleashed
the kind of day that terrifies priests and police
the kind of day that ends up in poems like these

I was walking along, just minding my own business
when a heard a noise, terrifying in bigness
it could have been robots having a riot
or possibly bears eating aeroplane pilots
or maybe werewolves learning to breakdance
or perhaps yetis who were all getting brain transplants

The noise was emanating from inside a nearby old warehouse
I approached the door, quiet as a church mouse
I summoned my courage, and eased it gently open
my jaw dropped to the floor when I saw what caused the commotion

Josh Donellan

This is a spell to make your imagination grow
It isn't quite finished yet. You'll have to figure the rest out on your own. But don't worry, you're practically a master poet (aka word wizard) by now! Best of luck, try to not turn anyone into cane toads or carpet pythons (unless they REALLY deserve it).

19½ Spells Disguised as Poems

About the Author

photo by David Clarke

There is a rumour that Josh Donellan was raised by mutant wolves in the mountains of Eastern Transylvania, but this is a half-truth. Currently, he lives in a secret cave 500 feet beneath a second-hand bookstore in Brisbane where he is slowly assembling an army of robots to ~~take over the world~~ help old ladies with their shopping.

He was a 2015 Australian Poetry Slam finalist and winner of the 2015 Ruckus Poetry Slam grand final. He has performed at the Brisbane Festival, TedxBrisbane (twice), Sydney Writers' Festival, Brisbane Powerhouse, and some very prestigious basements. His latest novel, *Killing Adonis*, received a Kirkus Star when it was published in the USA.

He writes novels, plays, poems, video games, and also presents enormously popular talks and workshops on the art of writing at schools, universities, and festivals throughout Australia via the booking agency Speakers Ink.

About the Illustrator

Holly Eastwood aka Hollywould is an illustrator, artist, and part-time mermaid who grew up near the beach on the Sunshine Coast. From her studio in Brisbane she loves to draw and sculpt ponies, unicorns, rabbits, and other cute creatures that live in Hollywould Land, her Etsy shop. She loves cats the most, but she is so allergic that she's tried her best to forget about them. One day she hopes to return to the ocean and become a full-time mermaid, part-time illustrator, and crazy hypo-allergenic breed cat lady.

www.ingramcontent.com/pod-product-compliance
Lightning Source LLC
Chambersburg PA
CBHW071319080526
44587CB00018B/3277